HARRY LEARNS
FRENCH

Illustrated by Annabel Tempest
Written by Sue Finnie & Danièle Bourdais

Copyright © ticktock Entertainment Ltd 2007
First published in Great Britain in 2007 by ticktock Media Ltd.,
Unit 2, Orchard Business Centre, North Farm Road,
Tunbridge Wells, Kent, TN2 3XF

ticktock project editor: Ruth Owen
ticktock project designer: Emma Randall

Text by Sue Finnie and Danièle Bourdais
Illustrations by Annabel Tempest

ISBN 978 1 84696 651 4 pbk

Printed in China

Bonjour!

Welcome to France. This book is your ticket on a whistle-stop tour of this beautiful country, and a great introduction to the French language.

1 Read

Follow Harry and Léa's adventures in France as they go to the beach, visit a farm and much more.

2 Learn

All the French words in this book are in **bold.** If you want to find out what they mean, turn to the handy phrasebook on pages 30 and 31. To help you speak French, there is also an easy-to-follow guide to pronunciation.

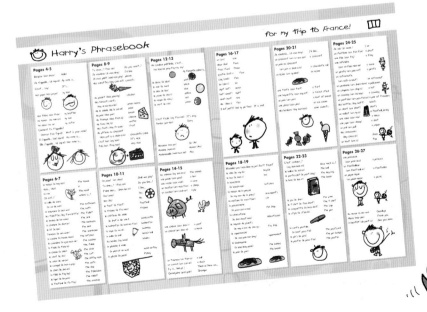

- **SORTIE** ▸▸
- **ARRIVÉES** ▴▾
- **RENSEIGNEMENTS** ◂◂
- **DÉPARTS** ◂◂
- **TRAINS** ▸▸
- **AUTOBUS** ▸▸
- **TAXIS** ▸▸
- **TOILETTES** ▾▾

Harry can't believe he's already in France! He loved being in the plane, on top of the clouds. Now he is going to meet Léa Bertin and her family. He'll be staying with them for a week.

What will he say? It's lucky he has a phrasebook to help him. It will come in handy – it will help you too!

"Bonjour, Harry!" says a voice near him. It must be Léa saying hello! **"Je m'appelle Léa!"** says the girl. Yes, it is Léa. **"Bonjour!"** says Harry excitedly as he is introduced to her family.

SORTIE

C'est mon papa.

C'est ma maman.

C'est ma sœur, Zoé.

C'est ma sœur, Chloé.

C'est mon frère, Louis.

How would you say your name in French?

Je m'appelle...

5

"C'est la maison!" says Monsieur Bertin, pointing at the house. Léa can't wait to show Harry her pets. There is Minou the cat, Jeannot the pet rabbit, and Filou the dog. But Filou is nowhere to be seen. *"Où est Filou?"* asks Léa.

Can you find Filou?

Filou est dans...

la salle de bains

le lavabo

la baignoire

les toilettes

l'armoire

le lit

la chambre

la cuisine

la cuisinière

la table

la chaise

Le chat est dans la cuisine.

le salon

le canapé

la télé

le fauteuil

Le lapin est dans le salon.

It's lunchtime. At first, Harry doesn't feel very hungry.
"Tu veux des carottes?" asks Madame Bertin.
He's not sure he wants any carrots, he doesn't have them
like that at home. Just a bit to try then... Mmm, yummy!

Je voudrais des carottes s'il vous plaît.

des carottes

de l'eau

de la salade

du pain

du gâteau au chocolat

des fruits

du poulet

des haricots verts

du fromage

He'd like more carrots, and chicken,
and green beans too, and salad,
and cheese, and bread...

...and lots of chocolate cake! Harry really, really loves chocolate!
"C'est bon?" asks Madame Bertin. Oh, yes, it's nice, very nice!
"C'est très bon!" says Harry, with a chocolate-covered smile on his chocolate-covered face!

Mmm, c'est bon!

Look at the table and say what you would like for lunch.

Je voudrais...

Next day it is warm and sunny, perfect for going to the beach. **"On joue?"** asks Léa. Good idea, let's play! Harry can't wait to show off his football skills to his new friend! **"Tu aimes bien le foot?"** he asks. **"Non"** replies Léa.

le foot

le badminton

le frisbee

le château de sable

Harry can't believe it: Léa doesn't like football! **"Tu aimes bien les boules?"** asks Léa. **"Oui, j'aime bien les boules,"** Harry says nodding, although he's not quite sure how to play!

la planche à voile

la nage

les boules

la pêche

la balle

Look at the beach and say what you like doing.

J'aime bien...

Léa shows Harry how to play boules: first you throw the little black ball and then you throw the bigger ones as close to it as possible. The person who throws the nearest ball wins a point. Harry plays with the red and blue balls. Léa plays with the yellow and green balls. Who wins the point?

What is your favourite colour?

Ma couleur préférée, c'est...

Oh no! Harry's boule has landed in the ice cream! The man looks really cross. Harry's very sorry. **"Pardon, monsieur!"**, he apologises. If only Léa would come and help him out!

But Léa is too busy laughing!

un cheval

un canard

une chèvre

une poule

14

The next day, Harry and Léa go to the farm belonging to Léa's grandpa. Harry is very excited. **"Tu aimes les animaux?,"** asks Léa. Harry loves animals, and can't wait to explore **Grand-père** Bertin's farm.

un taureau

un cochon

un mouton

une vache

What animals can you see?

Il y a...

Harry goes exploring. There are hens everywhere, and plenty of eggs to collect.
Harry wonders how many he'll find: ***"Un, deux, trois, quatre, cinq,***
six, sept, huit, neuf, dix!" Ten eggs!

Grand-père takes Léa to see some cute little piglets, just two days old. Léa picks one up. **"Il est petit!"** Yes, it is tiny. But not all farm animals are tiny and cute. Harry is looking at the bull. **"Il est gros!"** he laughs.

How many piglets can you count?

Un, deux...

The bull is big, VERY big and he looks cross, VERY cross! Run, Filou!

Saturday the 14th of July is a special day in France. It is the French National Day. To celebrate, Madame Bertin is organising a picnic for the children. She asks Harry and Léa to do some shopping in the village. **"N'oubliez pas le pain!"** she repeats. They must not forget the bread, it is very important.

la boucherie

la maison de la presse

LA POISSONNERIE

la charcuterie

le vélo

la voiture

Harry looks at all the shops along the main street. They look a bit different from those at home and he'd love to have a look in all of them.

Which shop would sell fish? A magazine? Some apples?

le magasin de jouets

le supermarché

la boulangerie

le bus

Harry can't believe his eyes when he sees all the lovely things in the **boulangerie**, especially the chocolate cakes. Léa buys lots of treats for the picnic.

des bonbons

Je voudrais une tarte, deux éclairs et des bonbons, s'il vous plaît.

une glace

When their basket is full, Léa and Harry head home. Madame Bertin will be very pleased with them. Or will she? Haven't they forgotten something, one very important thing?

Oui, mademoiselle.

une baguette

un pain

une tarte

un pain au chocolat

un croissant

un éclair

Which of these things would you like?

Je voudrais...

How would you ask how much something costs?

C'est combien...?

After going back to get the bread from the **boulangerie,** they pop into the **magasin de jouet.** Harry loves toys shops, and would just love to get that brilliant football in the window. But first, he wants to buy presents for all his family and friends.

le ballon

la carte postale

le t-shirt

la casquette

le stylo

le porte-clef

le pins

le jeu

le livre

le poster

Harry finds lots of lovely things for everyone. As he's got a bit of money left, he wants to know how much the football is. **"C'est combien, le ballon?"** he asks. It costs six euros. **"Un, deux, trois, quatre..."** Oh no, he hasn't got enough! He is almost tempted to give back the present for his sister!

Choose a costume for a fancy dress party!

Je suis...

The rest of the way home, Harry can't stop thinking about the football. Then, just in front of Léa's house, they see a group of Léa's friends, all out in fancy dress. **"Je suis un fantôme!"** says a familiar voice.

une fée

un pirate

un fantôme

un gendarme

un astronaute

une infirmière

un cowboy

Harry remembers that the picnic today is a fancy dress picnic!

Harry and Léa run in to choose their costumes. Harry looks at all the clothes on the bed. What are Harry and Léa going to be?

une robe

ne veste

un maillot

un chapeau

une jupe

un haut

des bottes

un pantalon

un pull

un short

des chaussures

As Harry the footballer and Princess Léa tuck into the delicious food at the picnic, Harry realises that he is going home tomorrow. The week in France has gone by in a flash.

The beach, the farm, the picnic...

un pique-nique

une princesse

un footballeur

His Mum and Dad won't believe how many French words he has learnt!

At the airport, Harry gives Monsieur and Madame Bertin
a kiss on each cheek and thanks them:
"Au revoir, monsieur, au revoir, madame... merci!"
Léa has a surprise for Harry. It's the football, the one Harry wanted
so much! **"Oh merci, Léa, merci!"** beams Harry.

Harry would love to
come back to France next
year, to see Léa and her family.
In his loudest voice, he calls out with
a last wave:**"À bientôt!"**
See you again soon!

My French Holiday Scrapbook

Léa's village

French money is
called the Euro.

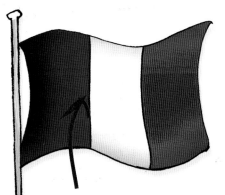

The French flag is
called the Tricolore.

French stamps

The Eiffel Tower is in Paris, the capital of France.

LUNDI	I met Léa and her family. Lovely lunch!
MARDI	A day at the beach (played boules!).
MERCREDI	Visit to Grand-père Bertin's farm.
JEUDI	Helped count chicken's eggs.
VENDREDI	A day at the beach.
SAMEDI	French National Day – Bastille Day: shopping, picnic, fancy dress party.
DIMANCHE	Time to go home!

France

France is famous for its lovely food and cakes.

Why not make a scrapbook after your next holiday?

Harry's Phrasebook

Pages 4-5

Bonjour (bon-shoor)	Hello!
Je m'appelle... (sh map-el)	My name is...
C'est... (say)	It's...
mon papa (mon pa-pa)	my dad

mon frère (mon frair)	my brother
ma maman (ma mam-on)	my mum
ma sœur (ma sir)	my sister

Comment tu t'appelles? (kom-on too tap-el)	What is your name?
Il s'appelle... (eel sap-el)	His name is...
Elle s'appelle... (el sap-el)	Her name is...

Pages 6-7

la maison (la may-zon)	the house
dans... (don)	in
la rue	the road
Où est...?	where is...?
la salle de bains (la sal de ban)	the bathroom
la baignoire (la ben-wa)	the bath
les toilettes (ley twa-lette)	the toilet
le lavabo (le lav-a-bo)	the sink
la chambre (la shom-br)	the bedroom
le lit (le lee)	the bed
l'armoire (le arm-warr)	the wardrobe
la cuisine (la kwee-zeen)	the kitchen
la cuisinière (la quiz-een-air)	the cooker
la table (la tarb-la)	the table
la chaise (la shez)	the chair
le chat (le sha)	the cat
le salon (le sal-on)	the sitting room
le canapé (le kan-a-pay)	the sofa
le chien (le she-an)	the dog
la télé (la tay-lay)	the television
le lapin (le lar-pan)	the rabbit
le fauteuil (le fo-toy)	the armchair

Pages 8-9

Tu veux...? (too ver)	Do you want...?
Je voudrais (sh voo-dray)	I'd like
s'il vous plaît (seel-voo play)	please
des carottes (day carr-ot)	carrots

du poulet (doo poo-lay)	chicken
des haricots verts (day ar-ee-ko-vair)	green beans
de la salade (de la sal-ad)	salad
du pain (doo pan)	bread
du fromage (doo from-aj)	cheese
de l'eau (de lo)	water
des fruits (day fr-wee)	fruit
du gâteau au chocolat (doo gat-o o shok-o-la)	chocolate cake
c'est bon (say bon)	It's nice
très bon (tray bon)	very nice

Pages 10-11

On joue? (on shoo)	Shall we play?
Tu aimes...? (too em)	Do you like...?
J'aime bien... (shem be-an)	I like...
Oui (wee)	Yes
Non (No)	No
le foot (le foot)	football
le frisbee (le fris-bee)	frisbee
le château de sable (le shat-o de sab-l)	sandcastle
le badminton (le bad-min-ton)	badminton
la nage (la na-sh)	swimming
la balle (la bal)	beach ball
les boules (lay bool)	boules
la planche à voile (la plon-sh av-wal)	wind-surfing
la pêche (la pesh)	fishing

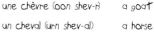

Pages 12-13

Ma couleur préférée, c'est...
(ma koo-lur pray-fay-ray say)

My favourite colour is...

le blanc (le blon)	white
le noir (le nwa)	black
le bleu (le blur)	blue
le jaune (le sho-n)	yellow
le rouge (le roo-j)	red
le vert (le vair)	green

C'est facile (say fass-eel)	It's easy
Pardon (par-don)	Sorry
Monsieur (mas-yur)	Sir (Mr)

Madame (mad-am)	Madam (Mrs)
Mademoiselle (mad-mwa-zel)	Miss

Pages 14-15

les animaux (lay zan-im-o)	the animals
une poule (oon pool)	a hen
une vache (oon vash)	a cow
un mouton (urn moo-ton)	a sheep
un cochon (urn cosh-on)	a pig

une chèvre (oon shev-r)	a goat
un cheval (urn shev-al)	a horse

un taureau (un torr-o)	a bull
un canard (urn can-ar)	a duck
Il y a... (eel-ya)	There is/There are
Grand-père (gron-pair)	Grandpa

for my trip to France!

Pages 16-17

(urn)	one
...x (dur)	two
...is (twa)	three
...tre (kat-r)	four
...q (sank)	five
...(see-s)	six
...t (set)	seven
...t (weet)	eight
...f (nurf)	nine
...(dee-s)	ten
...st petit (eel ay pe-tee)	It is small
...st gros (eel ay gro)	It is big

Pages 18-19

...ubliez pas (noo-blee-ay pa)	Don't forget
...vélo (le vay-lo)	a bicycle
...bus (le boo-s)	a bus
la boucherie (la boosh-ree)	the butchers
...maison de la presse (la may-zon de la press)	the newsagents
...voiture (la vwa-toor)	a car
...poissonnerie (la pwa-son-a-ree)	the fish shop
...charcuterie (la shar-koot-ree)	the delicatessen
...magasin de jouets (le mag-a-zan de sho-ay)	the toy shop
...supermarché (le soo-pair-mar-shay)	the supermarket
...boulangerie (la boo-long-gerie)	the bakers
...pain (le pan)	the bread

Pages 20-21

Je voudrais... (sh voo-dray)	I'd like...
un croissant (urn cr-wa-son)	a croissant
un pain au chocolat (urn pan o shok-o-la)	a chocolate roll
un éclair (urn ay-klair)	an eclair

une tarte (oon tart)	a tart
une baguette (oon bag-et)	a French stick
un pain (urn pan)	a loaf of bread
une glace (oon glas)	an ice cream
des bonbons (day bon-bon)	some sweets

Pages 22-23

C'est combien...? (say kom-bee-an)	How much is...?
le ballon (le bal-on)	the ball
le porte-clef (le port-klay)	the key-ring
le livre (le lee-vr)	the book

le jeu (le shur)	the game
le t-shirt (le tee-shurt)	the t-shirt
la casquette (la kass-ket)	the cap
le stylo (le stee-lo)	the pen

la carte postale (la kart poss-tal)	the postcard
le pins (le pinz)	the badges
le poster (le poss-tair)	the poster

Pages 24-25

Je suis... (sh swee)	I am...
un fantôme (urn fon-tom)	a ghost
une fée (oon fay)	a fairy
une infirmière (oon an-feer-mee-air)	a nurse
un pirate (urn pee-rat)	a pirate
un astronaute (urn astr-o-naut)	an astronaut
un gendarme (urn sharn-darm)	a policeman
un chapeau (urn shap-o)	a hat
un cowboy (urn ko-boy)	a cowboy
un pantalon (urn pon-tal-on)	a pair of trousers
des bottes (day bott)	boots
un short (urn short)	a pair of shorts
un maillot (urn my-o)	a football shirt
une robe (oon rob)	a dress
une jupe (oon shoop)	a skirt
un pull (urn pull)	a jumper
des chaussures (dey chass-er)	shoes
un haut (unn o)	a top

Pages 26-27

une princesse (oon pran-sess)	a princess
un footballeur (urn foot-ball-un)	a footballer
un pique-nique (un peek-neek)	a picnic

Au revoir (o-rev-wa)	Goodbye
Merci (mair-see)	Thank you
à bientôt (ab-yant-o)	See you soon

1

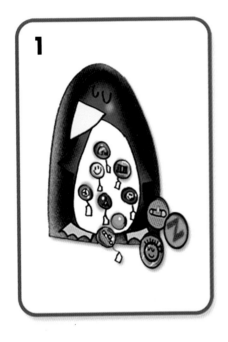

2

3

un maillot

le vélo

le chien

le livre

la chaise

le pins

4

5

6